Personal reflections, practical advice, and inspirational stories to help you on your journey

Kindly, Michelle

Michelle Trong Perrin-Steinberg

Kindly, Michelle: Personal reflections, practical advice, and inspirational stories to help you on your journey is a work of my own creation.

The information in this book was correct at the time of publication, and the Author does not assume any liability for loss or damage caused by errors or omissions, again, this is my perspective, opinion, and experience, so it has been written as such.

Copyright © 2024 by Michelle Trong Perrin-Steinberg

All rights reserved.

No part of this book may be reproduced or transmitted in any form or by any means, electronic or mechanical, including photocopying, recording, or by any information and retrieval systems, without the written permission of the Author and/or Publisher, except where permitted by law.

Editing & Cover Design by megs thompson — *www.megswrites.com*

ISBN - 978-1-961185-69-2 (paperback)
ISBN – 978-1-961185-68-5 (ebook)

www.inomniaparatuspublishing.com

This book is dedicated to my Mom and Dad. I love you. Thank you for everything. Who I am is because I had you both as parents and a God who was and is always with us.

It is also dedicated to my only child, Brandon Perrin Steinberg. God blessed me because I get to be your Mom. Remember to make your dreams come true! I can't wait to see how God continues to use you to make an impact in the world for the better. You are going to do remarkable things my son. I love you!

Note to the Reader

This book is for all of the dreamers in the world who want to make their own dreams come true.

Within these pages, I'm sharing my own experiences in hopes of helping to inspire, uplift, support, and encourage you on your journey towards something better.

Kindly,

Michelle

Table of Contents

Introduction 1

Different is a Blessing 5

Family Is Everything 15

Becoming A Lawyer 21

The Importance of Speaking Up 31

Actionable Steps for You 35

Key Takeaways 57

Additional Resources 61

About the Author 65

Acknowledgment 67

Kindly, Michelle

Introduction

Maybe you're just taking off your cap and gown after graduating high school, college, law school or other graduate school, in shock like a deer in headlights, overwhelmed by the number of choices and decisions you're now faced with making. Or perhaps you've been a member of 'the real world' for a while now but haven't yet found where you fit; what seems right, what fills your cup, and what makes getting up less of a chore and more of an adventure.

This book, these ideas, are meant for you.

You're not alone. Many well-adjusted adults were once (and may still be) right where you are now. Feeling the things you are and reeling at the overwhelming nature of the fast-paced world around us. But I'm here to tell you that it's going to be okay.

And, while you may be feeling like an oddball right now, those things that set you apart

from the crowd, the factors and attributes that make you, you, are also your superpowers. It's more important now than ever before in our history, that we share our unique voices, perspectives, opinions, beliefs, and experiences with the world.

A big part of my life, both personally and professionally, is that we each, as individuals, take accountability for uncovering, exploring, and recognizing what our own personal values are. When deciding on a future job opportunity or career plan, no matter how amazing a position or career may look on TV, on paper, or sound during an interview, if the organization's values don't align with your own, no salary, corner/remote office, or bonus package is going to satisfy your desires.

Now, before we really get into the good stuff, allow me to introduce myself.

I'm Michelle, a regulatory compliance lawyer with 20 years of experience in various industries while also acting as an advisory board member for Women, Influence, and Power in Law (WIPL); as well as an executive board member of the Syracuse University Law Alumni Association (SULAA).

Personally, I'm a wife, a boy mom, a daughter, a friend, and a dog mom who loves spending my free time with my family and friends, reading a good book, watching a movie, or exploring new things.

One thing that remains true in all areas of my life is my passion for bringing people together. Think networking but in the most authentic, genuine, and creative way you can imagine. I'm that person who meets someone at a spontaneous dinner party, and quickly connects them with another friend who I know they need to meet. This is just a part of my fundamental nature, an innate desire to connect. Regardless of where we are in the world, life is so much better, exciting, and fulfilling when we're able to see others for the ways in which we're different as well as similar and connect.

I've always seen the importance of putting people first, which I know stems from watching how my parents valued and prioritized not only our family, but our church community, friends, and neighbors. I grew up knowing that there was something bigger than just worrying about myself. Now, as an adult, I still recognize that while earning accolades for my own accomplishments is great, what really excites me is seeing the things that the organization and teams I'm a part of can achieve. I'm a firm believer in the mantra that a rising tide lifts all boats.

Kindly, Michelle

Within the following pages, I hope to inspire and empower <u>you</u> to explore the countless possibilities available on your own personal and professional journey, focusing not on simply making a living, but making a difference: tapping into your natural abilities, upholding your personal values, and acting as a lighthouse for future generations.

Ready? Let's go!

Michelle Trong Perrin-Steinberg

Kindly, Michelle

Different is a Blessing

My story starts in El Paso, Texas on Fort Bliss, a military base where I lived for only a few months before my Dad was assigned to a new Army base in Germany, which would become the first of many international assignments; opportunities for me to travel the world, explore different cultures, and begin the process of figuring out who I was and who I would become.

One of my favorite photos of Dad & I

As the only child of an African American father and a Vietnamese mother, I grew up knowing that I was a little different. Growing up, no matter where we lived, being biracial had a large impact on my identity. The black kids at school never thought I was black enough to hang out with them, and the Asian kids didn't think I looked Asian enough. Luckily, I've been blessed with amazing parents who both assured me that what mattered most at the end of the day was that I was proud of who I was, and they provided me with a spiritual and cultural backbone at home. This experience lit a fire in my belly to create a place for everyone to feel like they can belong, connect, and grow. This is something I've carried with me throughout grade school, my higher education, and workplaces, and now it factors largely into the career choices I've made and continue to make.

Added to my bi-racial upbringing was the excitement of being part of a military family, which meant that while most of the kids my age grew up living in the same house, with the same friends, and going to the same schools, I moved frequently, starting over more times than I can remember in a new place, with new people, culture, languages, and food. This also meant that making friends became one of my superpowers. I learned quickly that the best way to settle into a new place was to get to know those around me. And the best way to do that was to ask them questions about what they liked to do; listening to what they shared and finding places where we had commonalities.

One of the easiest ways to connect with strangers *(aka future friends)* was through pop culture and music. I knew from a young age that music transcended different cultures, and no matter where we lived, whether in the United States or internationally, everyone listened to music, and it was something people of all ages could talk about. Think about your current favorite artists, bands, songs, or albums. Don't you just love it when someone asks you what you're listening to? There's nothing quite like the excitement we experience when we're talking about our favorite musical groups.

Kindergarten Class Photo

My favorite childhood photo in my favorite dress

In many of the places my Dad was stationed, instead of living on the military base surrounded by other military families, my parents opted for us to live off base, providing me with a much more immersive experience than if I had spent my days on the military base. These experiences exposed me to countless different cultures, languages, and beliefs, and encouraged me to stay adaptable and flexible while also discovering and honing my own self-confidence and foundation of what values I hold dear.

By the time I was ready to graduate from high school I had already attended 9 different schools, and while you may think they would all run together, I can clearly remember significant experiences at each one.

After a few years in Germany, Buren and Lobberich specifically, my Dad's work brought us back to the US and we landed in Hampton, VA, where I attended Fox Hill Private School for kindergarten and first grade. This is where I first learned how to swim, something I still enjoy today, and was the only private school I would ever attend.

2nd Grade Class Photo

I attended Barcroft Elementary School in Arlington, VA for 2nd and 3rd grades. This school will always hold a special place in my heart because it's where I first discovered the joys of reading. I joined a handful of different book clubs and devoured everything I could get my hands on. This love of reading has helped me so much - being able to communicate more effectively and analyze with more information has served me well throughout my life. At the same time, I also realized how much I disliked math!

4th Grade Softball Team Photo

From Virginia we moved to Fort Leavenworth, Kansas, where I attended Eisenhower Elementary School for 4th grade. This year was one of my favorites because I was blessed with an absolutely amazing teacher who helped make things like spelling seem like fun and I found a love for spelling words. I joined Girl Scouts here, and in my spare time, mastered the art of riding my bike and roller skating. I would ride my bike and roller skate everywhere!

The next year was a challenging one for my family. Dad was stationed in South Korea for the first of his two years there and it was what the Army called a *'hardship'* tour because his family (Mom and I) weren't allowed to join him for the first year. Mom and Dad made the decision that until we could join Dad in South Korea the following year, we would move to Novato, CA to live with my uncle, aunt, and cousin. My uncle and cousin had previously escaped Vietnam as boat refugees and welcomed Mom and I to their home with open arms. I attended Lynwood Elementary School for 5th grade and was excited to be able to explore my newfound independence by riding my bike to and from school and visiting the public library where my cousin worked. I started learning how to cook while we were in California, something I enjoyed at the time, and wish I had kept up with as I got older. For some reason, now I don't really spend much time cooking although I enjoy preparing special meals like Thanksgiving for my family.

Mom and I were able to join Dad in South Korea just in time for me to start 6th grade at Seoul American Elementary School, A Department of Defense School in Yongsan, South Korea. It was here that I first learned how to play the flute, something I continued with through high school. While we were in South Korea, I remember my parents throwing me the best birthday party, and I was ecstatic to unwrap what would become my favorite present, my very own New Kids on the Block cassette tape! My parents loved taking day trips to explore our new home, try new foods, and learn everything we could about Korean culture. I also went skiing for the first time in South Korea, and discovered The Babysitters Club book series, which I read in its entirety!

Huntsville High School Marching Band

After Dad's second year in South Korea was finished, we all moved to Huntsville, AL where I attended Westlawn Middle School for 7th and 8th grades. I excelled through my last 2 years of middle school, taking talented and gifted classes and earning a place on the honor roll. I sang in the school choir while continuing to sharpen my skills on the flute.

While we were living in Huntsville, my parents made the decision to sponsor nearly 20 of my mom's family members from Vietnam. This was something my Mom and Dad had been talking about for ages since they were first married, and it came as no surprise to me that it was actually happening. Both of my parents are the kind of people who do what they say they will, honoring their commitments to themselves and others, something I'm thankful they imparted to me. While this was definitely something big and exciting it was also a huge shock to life as I knew it. I was no longer an only child with the full attention of my loving and devoted parents. I was now sharing not only my home but my parents' time with 20 extended family members, none of whom spoke much English at the time. Suddenly, the little trips my Dad and I took to the local store were shared with my cousins. Seeing the sacrifices my parents made; that they were willing and eager to make, in order to help other members of the family to have a better life, taught me that no matter what, family always comes first.

Family Vacation To Six Flags

The months leading up to my new family's arrival were hectic and filled with chores and errands to get everything set up to hopefully make their new home one that was comfortable and welcoming after their long trip. Dad spent countless hours filling out pages and pages of official forms and paperwork for each member of the family that was making the move. My parents even went so far as to purchase a second home for them to call their own, as well as a large commercial building, where they could earn a living. My Aunt started an alterations shop there and within only a few years' time, she was able to buy her own home, as well as purchasing the commercial building from Mom and Dad. She still owns the building and runs her successful alterations shop from there to this day! She is an inspiration to anyone wanting to come to America to have a better life.

If I'm being completely honest, when my 20 family members moved to the United States, it was not an easy change and I didn't always act in the most mature way, something that I am embarrassed about. There's one occasion that sticks out in my memories the most. It had been a seemingly normal day at middle school until it was time for lunch. My cousins had packed a sack lunch with the foods they were used to eating, however, they weren't things that our classmates were used to seeing or smelling. Instead of sticking up for my cousins, I opted to stay quiet and mind my own business, wanting to do everything I could to distance myself from them. Then, when it came time to head home for the day, my friends and I were all seated on the bus, ready to go, when the driver asked, "Are we missing anyone?" I knew that one of my cousins wasn't yet on the bus, but instead of speaking up, I held my tongue, while another cousin said that her brother was missing. I told the bus driver to leave him, and the bus driver did. When I arrived home, without one of my cousins, my Mom and Dad were not impressed and my Mom left the house to go pick up my cousin. I got an earful that night and my parents were very disappointed in me, not to mention my cousin who had cried the whole way home since we had left her brother at school.

It wasn't long before I started to see how what my parents were doing, the sacrifices they were making, was having an impact on not only my aunts and uncles, but their children, my cousins, providing them with an opportunity to better themselves and achieve a better life than they may have had if they'd stayed in Vietnam. It's so amazing because now, decades later, my cousins, all of them are college graduates with successful careers as engineers and medical professionals, some own their own businesses and they have started families of their own, raising their own children. This is something I carry with me throughout my day-to-day life at work; the knowledge that sometimes even a single decision can help drastically improve the life of someone else. At the end of the day, what matters most isn't what's best for just me, but for my family, the community, and the team. One thing I always remind myself and others of is the importance of building bridges.

We stayed in Huntsville through my freshman year of high school, and I attended Huntsville High School on a waiver, meaning that we didn't live in the right school zone for me to attend, but with the support of my parents and an appeal to the school board, we made it happen. I had a great English teacher at Huntsville High, who really helped strengthen my already enormous love for reading and writing. I continued playing the flute, this time in both orchestra and the school marching band. I also discovered keyboarding (typing on a traditional typewriter), which was a blast. I loved learning how to type super-fast, and this is definitely a skill that's continued to help me throughout my professional life.

From Alabama we moved back to Arlington, VA where I attended Wakefield High School for 10th grade. This was a very diverse school which I loved because I enjoyed getting to connect with so many people from different backgrounds and cultures. I earned a varsity letter for playing the flute, as well as participating in numerous local music competitions earning the highest scores possible for flute soloist or duets, which felt amazing. I was blessed to have a phenomenal math teacher who helped me believe in myself so much that I started enjoying math class and discovered that I was actually pretty good at it with hard work and focused attention. I joined the National Junior Honor Society as well as learned how to drive in summer school. 10th grade was a pretty exciting and monumental year for me.

I finished my last 2 years of high school in Madison, AL, at Bob Jones High School, a blue-ribbon school (the only one in our area). While keeping my grades up I also got my first real job (aka paid position) working at Applebees in the evenings and on the weekends. During this time, my family and I decided to host a Russian exchange student, which was a unique experience that my high school sponsored. I also got the chance to travel to Azov, Russia and stay with a Russian host family for a few weeks. During this time, I participated in an ecological study. Spending time in Russia is something I will always remember. I enrolled in college courses the summer before my senior year and had the time of my life living in Birmingham. I knew right then and there that I was going to love being a college student, and after graduating within the top 10% of my class, I was ready to start the next chapter of my life.

High School Graduation

While I excelled at school and in the creative outlets I pursued, there were definitely still areas of my life that reflected my age and immaturity. One such situation that my parents will never let me forget started with my getting a traffic ticket while still in high school. Instead of telling my parents about the infraction, when it happened, I tucked the ticket away in my wallet, sure that I would be able to take care of it on my own without Mom or Dad even knowing it had happened. However, I found myself on a trip and stuck at an airport overnight, with no way of getting back home in time to deal with the ticket. I can still clearly remember calling my parents from the airport, asking for their help to contact the police station, or traffic courthouse on my behalf, to explain what was going on since I would miss the court date and thus, there could be a warrant out for me. When Mom heard what was happening, she promptly hung up on me. I couldn't believe it. I called back and when Dad answered, I started explaining everything all over again. His response was only slightly better than Mom's. Instead of hanging up, he let me know in no uncertain terms that this was a great lesson for me to learn, that in life, no one else was going to clean up my messes.

Looking back now, as an adult, a wife, and a mother, I recognize what a *wonder woman* my Mom was and still is today. Our family was moving every few years, sometimes every year, but she always made it look seamless and easy. Dad was busy with work and getting situated in his new position, so Mom took care of setting up our new house, making it a home, getting a new job, getting me settled into a new school, and familiarizing herself with a new community. Now that I've had the experience of moving my own family of three plus a four-legged family member, I can fully understand how much work, patience, organization, and dedication go into making the experience one that's positive. Both  of my parents always made it a priority that I was able to enjoy being a kid without having to worry about the often-overwhelming adult things going on around me.

While I've always known my childhood was *different*, I've never considered myself better or worse than anyone else. I've always been competitive with myself, because I've wanted to do my best, make my parents proud, and achieve my own goals. But I've learned along the way that we don't get anywhere in life without the support of others. There will always be enough room for everyone, and I believe that God has a unique plan for me, and part of that is that I get to help support others in achieving their dreams. I can truly say that I've found the most satisfaction when I'm able to help others.

I also recognize that one of the primary reasons why change isn't something that scares me, is because of the huge life changes I witnessed within my own family. From my Mom, who moved from her home country to the United States all alone to my Dad, who made the decision to pursue and complete a college education, being the first in his family to do so, and of course, my 20-some family members who moved across the world without knowing exactly what was waiting for them when they landed in Alabama, but made the change anyway. I've been blessed to have such phenomenal role models throughout my life, making big changes and succeeding in the face of real-life challenges. I can't help but credit much of my fearlessness to all of them.

Michelle Trong Perrin-Steinberg

Family is Everything

Mom & Dad visiting us in Hawaii

I attribute much of who I am today, as well as what I've been able to accomplish both personally and professionally, to the examples set for me by my parents.

My Mom is one of the strongest, most fearless women I've ever met. She came to the US as an immigrant on January 26, 1972, moving to California from Vietnam. She was the first member of her family to come to America. Her older brother, my uncle, followed later in 1982. She worked multiple jobs while also taking courses to learn English, and soon found positions within the medical field to support herself. My Mom has never been afraid to make mistakes or take calculated risks; she's always had an innate drive to overcome any obstacle that may come up to create a better life for herself and her future family, even when it meant leaving everything she knew behind in Vietnam, to bet on herself.

My Mom grew up as one of the oldest of 16 children, with 11 biological and 5 adopted male siblings who were war orphans. She learned at an early age how to care for her younger brothers and sisters while also supporting her mother by doing chores around the house. When my Mom was growing up, girls in Vietnam were not allowed to continue their education past 5th or 6th grade. So, while her brothers continued going to school or got jobs to help support the family, my Mom, and other young women like my Mom, were tasked with learning to take care of the children and home. I know without a doubt that had my Mom been given the opportunity, she would have chosen to continue going to school. She was then, and still is today, an extremely smart woman who picks things up very quickly, teaching herself countless new skills anytime she stumbles across something that interests her. I saw this when she pivoted from the medical field to cosmetology. When I was in middle school, she went to school to learn cosmetology; completed the hours required; and passed her Boards. She wanted to achieve something and she did it. My Mom has always been a woman with a kind heart who shows love with even her smallest actions.

My Dad was raised by his father and grandmother in Gloucester, VA, and from a young age he felt an overwhelming love for his country. His older brother, my uncle, who he also grew up with in Gloucester, joined the Marines and fought in the Vietnam war (which would become the first of many wars my uncle served in throughout his career in the Marines). After participating in ROTC throughout college, Dad joined the Army as a Second Lieutenant and went on to serve 27 years in the military before retiring as a full-bird Colonel. As a devoted father, soldier, and man of God, my Dad is a true leader. I'm proud to say that many of the leadership skills I use today, in my own professional career, are ones that I learned from my father. My Dad grew up in the church, believing from a young age that his confidence and abilities were gifts from God, and meant to be shared with others. Like my Mom, Dad had never been one to give up or give in on his big dreams. Instead, he was eager to put in the hard work required to achieve success. My Dad was not only the first member of his family to earn a college

degree, but he was also one of the first African Americans to attend and graduate from the University of Virginia (UVA).

Mom and Dad first met when they were set up on a blind date by friends in Monterrey, California. After a few months of dating, my Mom became a Christian and my parents were married in a military chapel on the base where Dad was stationed at the time.

My parents have taught me countless life lessons, not only by their words, but more importantly through their actions. I grew up seeing firsthand that anything is possible if we set our minds to it and put in the work. While many children hear the age-old mantra *you can be anything you want when you grow up,* my parents showed me this every single day. They also instilled in me a desire to never give up, not even when faced with unimaginable setbacks or hurdles. They were prime examples of making the seemingly impossible, possible. Sometimes the first attempt at something doesn't work, but if you stay committed, adjust your approach, and believe in yourself, you really can do anything you set your mind to.

At the same time, no matter what I accomplished, whether it was learning a new skill, or bringing home a good grade, my parents always reminded me of the importance of staying humble and being kind even when chasing your dreams. My parents taught me to respect others and that each and every one of us is worthy of receiving respect, even in those interactions with seemingly difficult or uncomfortable people or circumstances. This is something that's been monumental in my professional life, working within different industries with a wide variety of personalities, learning styles, cultures, and environments.

Once I was old enough, my parents encouraged me to work, not only to learn the value of money, but responsibility, what it means to be part of a team, and time management. This has been instrumental not only in my professional life, but personally as well, especially when it comes to balancing my career with being a wife and a mother. I take great pride in the fact that I refuse to sacrifice my marriage or the joys of motherhood for anything. I always put my family first. Yes, my work schedule may look a little wonky - leaving in the afternoon to pick up my son from school and then getting back online after his bedtime to catch up on emails or to meet virtually with a colleague in another time zone, but I hold firm on taking time every evening, no matter what else is going on, to have dinner with my husband and son. This is a priority for me and is something I learned from my parents.

When I was in middle school, Dad encouraged me to go visit one of his older sisters, my aunt, cousins, and grandmother in Long Island, New York for a few weeks. It was a memorable experience for me because it gave me the opportunity to see how other family members lived and how their households ran. I still remember today that my cousin, who is the same age as me, was so much cooler than I was. At least that's how I saw her (and she is still the cool cousin to this day)! She lived in the *big city*, and got to go shopping at the mall, spending her money on whatever she wanted. During this trip, the big thing was a pair of all black Fila sneakers. After seeing how cool she looked in her new shoes, I was insanely jealous and knew that I needed a pair, too. Before leaving for the trip, Mom and Dad had sat me down and talked about the importance of budgeting the money I was bringing with me, to cover necessities as they came up. When we got home from the mall, with my super cool new black sneakers on my feet (which were actually a little bit too small, but since they didn't have my size, I bought the closest size they had because I "needed" them so badly), I called my Mom and Dad, telling them all about my purchase, which had completely depleted my funds, but made me happy! Needless to say, they were not as excited about my shoes as I was. Dad instructed my aunt to take me back to the mall the following day, to return the shoes. I was devastated, humiliated, and couldn't believe it was happening. Looking back now, I can see how my parents were teaching me a lesson about the importance of budgeting and making sure the *necessities* were taken care of before making purchases that I *wanted*. They also taught me that I should only buy something if it fits properly. What is the purpose of buying shoes that do not fit well? It is not a wise purchase.

From my earliest memories, I've known that my parents have wanted the best for me, and now, decades later, they continue to provide guidance and support when needed, to not only me; but my husband, who often seeks out advice and counsel from my Dad; and now my 10-year-old son Brandon, who seeks their advice all the time on a variety of topics. It makes me incredibly happy to see how much my parents delight in the very special relationship they have with my son; laughing and sharing stories from their own childhoods, which are so drastically different from his. My Mom and Dad continue to pour out wisdom, and I thank God every day that He blessed me with the very best parents. I know without a doubt that I would not be the person I am today without their unwavering love and support.

My parents have always and continue to show me through their own relationship what it means to choose a life partner who loves, respects, and genuinely desires the best for you no matter the situation. They taught me, without saying a word, the importance of choosing the right spouse and partner in life. As a career woman, I knew that my perfect partner would be someone who would support my dreams and ambitions, doing their best to not limit my growth. I'm beyond blessed that I found this and more in my husband, Brian. I've never questioned or doubted whether Brian wants the best for me. He understands when plans need to change, when I need to travel for work, to attend a conference, or speak at an event. He knows that there are times when I need to work late at night, or early in the morning. He shares the responsibilities of keeping our home running and is willing to take on more than his share of the parenting when necessary. My parents set the example for me, of what it can look like, to grow up in a home that has the foundation of a loving and supportive partnership, and I'm grateful that Brian and I are able to provide that same experience for our son.

When I reflect back on our relationship thus far, I'm reminded of the saying, *what's meant for you isn't going to miss you.* Years ago, I was living in Virginia and one of my friends from law school kept trying to convince me to come visit her in NYC for a long weekend. Sure, she wanted to spend time together but her primary goal was setting me up with *some guy*. A friend of her fiance's, and someone she was just certain, I needed to meet. But, I was busy in Virginia and had absolutely no desire to go to another city just to meet a guy. Fast forward to a year later and I'm in Texas for a full week, attending the traditional Indian wedding festivities for that same amazing friend. Before long, this handsome man was sitting next to me, and it turned out, this was the same guy she'd been trying to set me up with. Through hours of conversation we discovered that we both lived in Virginia, and had more in common than I had with anyone else I'd ever dated. When the festivities were done and everyone went home, we exchanged numbers, and once we were both back in Virginia, we arranged to go on our first official date (the next weekend). 6 months later we were engaged, and the rest, as they say, is history. Brian is without any hesitation or doubt, my person. And, I believe that we met exactly when, where, and how we were meant to, to begin the process of building a life together for our own family.

Our wedding on Oahu, HI in 2011

Kindly, Michelle

Becoming a Lawyer

For the longest time, I was positive that I was going to be a medical doctor when I grew up. It wasn't until my first year of college at UVA (yep, I followed in my Dad's footsteps and attended his alma mater), when I took a commercial law class that I decided I was more interested in than I was in biology, chemistry, or doing lab work. We didn't have any lawyers that were family friends, and I didn't actually know anyone that worked in the legal field, but I had confidence in my ability to learn everything I would need to be a successful lawyer, just like anyone else. And I decided to take the next steps to pursue this new path and dream.

College Graduation 2001

My Mom wanted me to stick with my pursuit of being a medical doctor. It had been her dream for me to become a doctor, simply because it's what I had been saying I wanted to be for as long as either of us could remember. She'd been encouraging me in that one direction my entire life, and then, I changed my mind and shifted my academic plans drastically. It's funny, even today Mom still jokes about how she wishes I had become a doctor. But, one of the great things about my Mom is that while she had her own thoughts and desires as far as what her only daughter would grow up to be, she is now and has always been fully supportive of whatever it is that I wanted to do; reminding me that what matters most is that I continue working hard for whatever it is I decide to pursue and that whatever it was, that it could support me and the life I wanted to have.

Dad told me that if I wanted to go to law school, he'd support my decision; however, he wanted to be sure that I understood it wasn't going to be easy. He warned me from the start

Michelle Trong Perrin-Steinberg

that I would have to work extra hard in all of my classes, as well as pass the bar exam when it came time. My parents had instilled in me from a very young age, the desire to always do the best, and be the best I can be. So, that's exactly what I set out to do.

My official journey to becoming a lawyer started right then and there. I started by applying for and completing as many externships and internships as I could, to gain a variety of experience in different legal settings (law firms, legal non-profits and organizations). I also decided to complete a pre-law summer program in California to confirm that law school was indeed something I wanted to pursue. After completing the pre-law summer program, I was confident that law school was the next step for me. I decided to continue my education at Syracuse University College of Law, enrolling in 2002.

While I followed my Dad to UVA, he actually followed me to Syracuse University, attending the Maxwell School of Citizenship and Public Affairs to first complete a National Security Studies program and then continuing on to obtain his Masters in Public Administration while I earned my law degree. We graduated from UVA 26 years apart but celebrated our mutual graduations from SU in 2005. I will always remember how my Dad was able to be there for special events such as my first oral argument in my first-year legal writing course. Dad and I have always been very close, and we share an even closer bond now, having graduated from the same undergraduate and graduate schools. We both share an immense amount of pride in being alumni from UVA and SU.

Law School 3L

The first year (1L year) of any law student is pretty typical; you take the required courses on Torts, Property, Contracts, Civil Procedure, Criminal Law, Constitutional Law, and Legal Research and Writing. After the 1L year, you are able to select the types of courses you are interested in and I enrolled in a variety of legal courses, hoping to find an area of law that stood out amongst the rest. I was still looking for that one *'thing'*, that one *'spark'* that gave me pause and made me want to settle down in a particular area of the law. Sadly, no matter how many different courses I took, or how many facets of the law I studied, I didn't find that passion I was looking for while I was in law school. So, after graduating in 2005, I opted to take a 1-year clerkship position with

Judge Lawrence M. Lawson, Assignment Judge at the Superior Court of New Jersey, Monmouth County.

To say that Judge Lawson was a trailblazer would be putting it lightly. Not only was he the first African American Assignment Judge (similar to a Chief Judge, or the highest-ranking Judge on the bench) for Monmouth County, but before this, he was the first African American Mayor of Neptune Township. Judge Lawson was also the first lawyer in his family (just like me) and was genuinely interested in sharing his experiences with me, a newly graduated, up-and-coming lawyer. The time I spent working with Judge Lawson was valuable beyond measure, and I highly recommend exploring clerkship opportunities to anyone who hasn't yet found their passion or spark in law school. During my clerkship, I was exposed to quite a few different areas of the law including land use, family law cases such as adoption, and criminal law cases such as Megan's Law tiering. Judge Lawson showed me firsthand what it means to be a good lawyer.

Swearing in Ceremony for The Virginia Bar

After my clerkship ended, I returned home to Virginia and started working in government contracts at Booz Allen Hamilton, a large federal government contractor. While working at Booz Allen, I was exposed for the first time to export control and international trade law. For those unfamiliar with the topics, you may be thinking, *"Big deal?"* But for me, this was that spark I had been looking for. I knew right away that this area of the law was what I wanted to focus on.

My next position was in aerospace and defense at SAIC, working at a business unit level, where I had some great leaders who took me under their wing, teaching me the foundations of export control compliance. My primary focus at the time was working on the day-to-day aspects of supporting programs with licensing and compliance. This taught me how to comprehensively read regulations and provided me with the practical experience of writing license applications and working with government submission tools.

After SAIC, I accepted a position working at the corporate level at The Boeing Company on the investigations side of things, evaluating whether there was a violation and if so, putting in place corrective measures to prevent future recurrences. This was more of a compliance role, looking into potential violations of non-compliance, and keeping an eye out for any gaps in the program. This provided me with experience in writing voluntary and self-disclosures to regulators and often hand-carrying correspondence to the State Department in DC. About this time, trade reform was happening, so I was busy learning all of the new changes.

After working at Boeing, I excitedly accepted a new position as a Mom to my amazing son Brandon. He was born in 2013, and I'll forever be grateful to have had the privilege of taking time away from the workforce, to focus instead on spending that special time with him. I had always wanted to be a mom and was beyond happy when I found out I was pregnant. As an only child myself, the idea of having a single child appealed to me, so I knew that I wanted to experience everything I could while being pregnant and after giving birth.

Our Growing Family

A close friend of mine had chosen to have a completely natural, drug-free birth with her child and after hearing about her natural birth experience, I knew right away that's what I wanted as well. No one in either my husband or my family had elected to proceed this way previously, so it was a new concept that took both of our families a bit of time to get used to. Brian and I completed *Bradley Natural Childbirth* and *Hypnobirthing* training, and through everything we learned I couldn't help thinking, "*This all just makes so much sense.*" When the time came and labor started, everything I had learned and practiced came into play and I was able to have Brandon in a birthing inn with the support of a midwife, 2 doulas, and my husband. It was an incredible experience and confirmed for both Brian and I that we could do hard things together!

Kindly, Michelle

Baby Brandon

Brandon was always a happy baby. Smiling, laughing, and very smart. He learned how to read at a very young age, and at 17 months, he started attending Montessori school. I had planned to stay home with him for 2 full years, but he let us know that he wanted to be around other kids his age and needed more stimulation. He thrived at Montessori and loved exploring how things worked. Something he's still captivated by today.

In 2020, when the pandemic happened, Brandon was in kindergarten, and it was so strange for him to be finishing school on Zoom. For 1st grade, Brian and I decided to homeschool Brandon using the Abeka Christian curriculum. I never thought that I would homeschool my child, but it was the best choice for us given the circumstances. That year turned out better than we would have thought! Brandon thrived with the Abeka curriculum, and Brian and I were excited to be his teachers. Brandon learned so much that year - including how to write in cursive!

As I write this, Brandon is now in his last year of elementary school, 5th grade. He's attended 4 different schools in 2 different states since starting kindergarten and has proven time and time again how resilient and adaptable he is. I am so proud of him!

When I did go back to the workforce, I jumped back in as Director of Export Control Compliance at a major research University — the University of Miami. This was the first time I wasn't working with a large export control compliance team; instead, I was working in higher education as an office of one. I no longer had a team or full-time, dedicated export control colleagues that I could count on for support. This

Brandon - 10 years old

Brian & I at a fun run I organized while at UM

was a real learning experience for me, and it was while in this position that I realized how much I thrive as part of a team, but I also embraced the responsibility of creating something and having the autonomy and authority to implement it. Part of my responsibility was to create and implement policies and procedures and to bring automation tools to the University. I also got the chance to submit my first-ever Office of Foreign Assets Control (OFAC) license to the US Department of the Treasury for a research boat to cruise into international waters. It was exciting and very different from anything I had done previously. I also spent a lot of time creating training and enablement to share knowledge across the University community on what export control and sanctions are and how they apply in a university setting. At this same time, there was much change happening within the Cuban Assets Control Regulation (CACR) and I found myself working with sanctions laws for the very first time.

I went on to work at Raytheon Technologies managing a large volume of licenses and experiencing what it was like to work through an on-site monitorship; to go through a compliance settlement; and the various reporting obligations and changes this brings in order to ultimately make a program stronger.

It was only then, after working at Raytheon and years after having graduated from law school, that I experienced what it was like to work within a traditional law firm setting, or *Law Firm Land* as I like to call it.

Now, a little background on why it was I never felt like law firm land was for me. Remember how I explained that growing up I didn't know any lawyers? Everything I knew about the law and legal proceedings was gleaned from television and movies until I was at UVA and started to complete externships and internships at law firms. TV and movies portrayed law firm attorneys as working and billing crazy hours, being extremely cut-throat, always chasing the next big case or paycheck, and not being particularly happy in the process. Even after I graduated from law school and held a few different positions, I heard from former classmates how unhappy they were in law firm land but wanted to stick it out to pay off student loans, or until they could land an in-house role. After I had been working for a number of years in-house, I started hearing from people just how abnormal it was that I started my career the way that I did - not in law firm land - that I opted to pursue a career outside of the traditional law firm setting. I heard it time and time again when I met new colleagues, interviewed for positions, or attended networking events that no one could believe that I had made the conscious choice to explore outside the box of what was expected of me. So, after working at Raytheon, and feeling like I may actually be missing out on something big, I decided to take a position within a law firm.

I met some amazing people in law firm land - top notch lawyers who were excellent advocates for their clients and the best in their field. I enjoyed the opportunity to support some truly great clients doing important work; however, I learned pretty quickly that *Law Firm Land* wasn't the right place for me. My issue was with the law firm model itself, which is primarily based on billable hours, and being what I saw as a "temporary problem solver" for a client. What I mean by that is that most of the clients a law firm represents already have their own in-house counsel who are engaged daily in the work of the company. Law firms or outside counsel were called in to help the client make the best decision possible - to be fully

informed when making a decision. But law firms and outside counsel generally came in only when there was a big transaction; a critical problem to solve, or when something really bad might happen or has happened. I've heard many say that if you want a legal answer, hire a law firm, but if you want a more holistic view, that's when you need in-house lawyers. Law firms and outside counsel fix the issue, and then typically do not hear from the client again unless something else major comes up. I was looking for *relationships* with my clients and working *collaboratively*. I knew I wanted to continue to support clients, but in a different way.

From law firm land, I was extended the invitation to join the management team of Deloitte's Global Trade Advisory practice group. It was a great experience to join a Big 4 consulting firm and support global clients of all shapes and sizes, from those just starting out, to some who were much more established, domestic and international. I was also able to travel quite a bit in this position, supporting clients everywhere from Bangkok to Brussels. What I enjoyed most though was that I was working as part of a team, all focused on the same goal of supporting our clients.

At Deloitte, I also had the opportunity to manage high-performing teams and act as a mentor to others. Many of the trade professionals I worked with while at Deloitte were more junior than I was, some even in their first role in trade compliance, so it was my responsibility to help coach them. This allowed me an amazing opportunity to support my colleagues through the process of finding and matching their skills to our client work, so they could grow personally and professionally, while best serving our clients. I got a lot of satisfaction coming alongside my junior colleagues to help them grow and continue to stay engaged with many of them and their career progress after Deloitte! I enjoy catching up with former Deloitte colleagues and sharing our successes since working together.

Then, at the start of the pandemic in April 2020, I was offered the opportunity to join SAP, a leader in enterprise resource planning software and technology company. I was worried, that it might not be the best idea to change jobs during such a turbulent time, like a global health pandemic, but I knew that I wanted the experience of working within the tech industry, stretching myself even further into the unknown, and with the support of my husband, I made what has turned out to be a really great decision. It's funny how sometimes the best opportunities present themselves when things are the most chaotic.

Over the past 4.5 years, I have been with SAP. My work involves collaborating with SAP's cloud business groups and functional teams; defining and implementing export control and trade sanctions policies; leading our role-based strategic enablement program; and advising on best practices. To my knowledge, I was the first person of color to be hired on the export control legal team and remain the only African American and bi-racial attorney on the team. I am also the first regional counsel hired for the team.

Looking back over my career thus far, I can see that in every role, I've focused on building relationships. This is key for me. My business is built on connections with people and over the years I have amassed an amazing network of legal, business, and compliance colleagues that I can count on for support and for whom I am happy to support. Being able to practice international trade in so many different sectors has given me such breadth and depth that my advice and counsel is unique, taking into consideration my nearly 20 years of practical experience. I'm able to bring a different perspective, something not many trade attorneys can do because many pick law firms or in-house and not both or pick one industry and do not explore a variety of industries like I have. Maybe this is why my parents call me their *unicorn*.

There is no harm in trying different things before settling on what it is you want to do with your life. You never know when a new opportunity may present itself, a new door might open, or a new path appears. Stay open to experiencing and learning what you can where you are now, but with your eyes on the horizon, keeping a look out for what might be coming next. I wouldn't change my own professional journey. Every position I've held, every company I've worked for, and every client I've supported, has taught me something, and it's all of those lessons that have allowed me to excel to where I am today.

Kindly, Michelle

The Importance of Speaking Up

In case you haven't picked up on it yet, I'm not someone who does well just sitting back and watching the world pass them by. I've always wanted to be involved in things, to experience as much as I can in life, and to learn from those who are a few steps ahead of me. This has led to me being involved in some pretty exciting opportunities and organizations most of which share a common focus of encouraging individuals of all backgrounds, cultures, races, beliefs, and experiences to speak up, stand up, and share their unique perspectives.

One of my biggest beliefs is that there needs to be greater representation of people of color, and women in general, in the legal profession and in the top leadership positions. You might say that I'm on a mission of sorts, to connect with other women and women of color and to encourage all of us to explore the limitless opportunities available to us.

I joined the Syracuse University Law Alumni Association (SULAA) Board of Directors in 2018 with the intention of determining how I might best be able to support diverse law students. I graduated in 2005, but in my time since law school, I didn't feel like I had really found a way to give back, at least not in the way I wanted to. When I joined SULAA, I had a vision of creating a committee whose focus was on developing an inclusion network. Thankfully, other alumni shared the same kind of goal, and together we were able to create the Inclusion Network, to serve diverse law students, as a committee of diverse law alumni, sharing our personal experiences, offering support, and providing career guidance. For many of us in the Inclusion Network, we were the first attorneys within our families, something we had in common with the law students we were serving. The law students expressed over and over again how valuable it was to have someone who looked like them, who had similar experiences to their own, and who were also blazing the trail in their own families, showing them that nothing was impossible.

In 2020, not only did we all experience a global health pandemic, but also a racial awakening and everything that came with it. Thankfully, the Inclusion Network was there to serve as a safe space for diverse law students and alumni to come together virtually. We hosted round table discussions and Zoom happy hours to encourage and foster a virtual community that allowed students to avoid feeling alone during such a tumultuous and uncertain time. The other alumni and I were also able to help support law students as they prepared for the bar exam and sent care packages with supplies to keep their spirits up.

Another reason why I was so interested in joining SULAA was to increase exposure given to the export control and trade sanctions practice area. When I was a law student, I didn't even know this career practice existed, and I realized that many law students today were still missing out on the same opportunity. It hadn't been until after I had graduated from law school and was working in government contracts that I stumbled upon export control regulations.

There are so many possibilities when it comes to practicing law, but oftentimes many career paths are overlooked during our law school years, which means that many law students are left not having found their desired focus until after graduation, once they've had a chance to put their education to work and explore what's out there. To do my part, I continue to sit on panels when I can, as well as speak at conferences and on podcasts to raise awareness about my unique area of the law.

I'm also on the Advisory Board for Women, Influence & Power in Law (WIPL), where my goal is to help identify and create opportunities for diverse panelists and speakers to join the speaker faculty at the annual WIPL conference. Through my involvement with WIPL, I've been able to help promote awareness and create countless opportunities for other women and women of color to have speaking opportunities. Often, these opportunities are related to international trade, but I also seek out panelists and speakers for other areas of the law. I believe it is important to incorporate diverse voices into panel discussions for a different perspective and to further the conversation. We should be

At the 2023 WIPL Conference with our Keynote Speaker, Brooke Shields.

At the 2024 WIPL Conference with our Keynote Speaker, Venus Williams.

unapologetic about who we are and how who we are influences our experiences, our thoughts, and our unique approach to solving problems.

When I first joined SAP, it was during the start of the pandemic on April 6, 2020. Everyone was working remotely from home, and when I received my new work laptop in the mail, my first thought was, "*This is great that I can be safe during the pandemic and work from home, but how am I going to build relationships with my new colleagues?*" My team was global with my direct manager located in Germany. I was living in the DC area, and because of the global restrictions in place, meeting in person was completely out of the question. I sent an email to the VP for North America Diversity, Equity, and Inclusion to ask her how I could get involved in the various employee network groups (ENGs) at the company. I wanted to find people who cared about the things I cared about. The next thing I knew, we were on a call for over an hour, and she invited me to join NADIC, the North America Diversity & Inclusion Council, whose focus is to continue to make, "DEI the DNA at SAP."

By joining NADIC, I was able to share my perspective on joining SAP during the start of a pandemic; and based on my on-boarding experience, the company instituted a Buddy program - where new hires could opt-in to receiving a DEI buddy to share the many resources SAP has to offer, including how to get engaged in the ENGs.

One of the reasons why I believe inclusion is so important within the field of export control and trade sanctions is that inclusive trade policies ensure that the trade laws and regulations being developed by the lawmakers take into consideration the unique impacts on women, people of color, and financially disadvantaged groups; thereby promoting fairness, and equity while encouraging more effective trade solutions. Ultimately, promoting diversity strengthens the effectiveness of any team, while also providing a safe space for all parties to feel seen, heard, and valued.

To succeed while working in law and most other industries, especially when most people in power do not look like you, it's important that you not let other people tell you who you are and what you can or can't do. Believe in yourself always. Keep moving forward. Don't give up. People will try to limit you and try to push you aside, wanting you to believe that where you are is "good enough," but you have to keep pursuing your dreams and don't ever settle for anything less than what you want.

There may be people who seek to do you harm, whether because they believe there isn't enough room for everyone to have a seat at the table (due to generational divides or otherwise), or perhaps they see something special in you that you don't yet see for yourself, and to stand out themselves, they seek to dull your shine. Whatever you do, continue to hold your head high. For myself, as a believer in Christ, I know that God takes it all and turns it around for my good. And I do not worry about what others are doing. I stay true to myself and keep moving forward. I also try to find those people who do support me. There are good people everywhere. Find them. And if you can't, be one. Be the good person who shines your light to help someone else. Remember, you can do hard things. You've already accomplished so much, and sometimes it's a matter of navigating an environment that isn't meant for you, to find the next best role where you'll be supported and set up to succeed.

Nothing will ever replace you owning your career. You have to do the work and be honest with yourself on what you really want. Be deliberate in how you intend to get there. Make a plan and achieve your goals. You can do it. You will have a fulfilling life if you put the work in and don't stop climbing. It helps to have others who are also driven around you. These people push you to continue striving and can celebrate with you when you reach closer and closer to your goals. I'm so thankful I have amazing people I've met along the way who encourage me and whom I can encourage. You know who you are - thank you!

Kindly, Michelle

Actionable Steps for You

I've always had a pretty solid level of self-esteem. While many of my peers have struggled with being comfortable in their own skin, both as children and for some still today as adults, I credit my innate level of confidence and self-awareness to the way my parents raised me. Yes, there were times when I was younger when I questioned my identity as a bi-racial kid and struggled with accepting myself. Still, I've always felt that I could talk with my parents about this, and they helped me to be proud of my ethnicity, and culture and always taught me to be proud of who I am.

I remember in grade school, seeing some of my classmates sitting alone, feeling left out by the *"cool kids"* or just not quite fitting in. I felt sad for them, that they were so attached to what other people thought of them, and whether they measured up to someone else's expectations. Whereas I knew that all of "this" was temporary. The drama that surrounded who was picked for which team, who brought what to eat for lunch, and who wore it better didn't warrant any real concern or worry on my part. It probably also helped that our family moved as often as we did, providing me with the chance to escape and start over again. It was no big deal for me, to start over again in a new place, make new friends, and explore new cultures. Remember, by the time I finished high school, I had attended 9 different schools! Besides, if things weren't the best, I only had to deal with it for a year before I would get to start over again somewhere else. I've always known that no matter how tough something might seem in the moment, it was in fact temporary, and I had much bigger things ahead of me in life.

You may be thinking; *Sure Michelle, this all sounds great and I'm glad you've found a career that interests you, but what about me? How do I do that for myself?*

First off let's talk about how you *should* be spending your time in your 20's. Explore. Grow. Try new things. Stop limiting yourself and choosing to pursue things based only on what other people are doing or saying you should do. Your 20's are for YOU. I took my 20's to travel, try different jobs, take a variety of classes, and do the inner work to prepare myself for the future. I figured out what I liked doing, and what I didn't. I explored how I might like to support myself financially, in order to create a life that I absolutely love living. I learned from my parents that while they had dreams for me, their only child, more than anything, they wanted me to follow NOT their footsteps, by my own. They encouraged me to take their advice, learn from the lessons they had taught me, but to also make my own mistakes. Your 20's are the time when you're meant to be figuring out what you like in life, and what you don't.

Alright, let's dig in.

Well, it all starts with putting in the work to uncover, explore & pursue what's going to be right for you.

Uncover

There is no getting around the fact that each and every individual is responsible for putting in the work to know themselves.

When I say, *know yourself*, I'm talking about finding a baseline for who you are, at your core. As described in the book **Sparked**, by Jonathan Fields, when you have a clear idea of who you are, really, you're more likely to feel a sense of purpose, experience a sense of flow, feel excited and energized, perform at your best, and genuinely believe that what you do in life matters. Start by asking yourself the questions on the following pages.

- What makes you tick?

- What are you most passionate about?

- What topics or activities interest you most?

- What are the core principles that guide your life?

- What do you want to be known for or remembered for?

- How do you work best?

- What projects or tasks make you feel most alive and excited?

- How do you get energized?

- What drains your energy?

- What kind of people do you like working with most?

- When you're being partnered up with someone for a project, what attributes are you most looking for?

- What kind of people do you surround yourself with in your personal life?

- Do you like to create or work on something pre-existing?

- Do you prefer to lead, or do you prefer to work behind the scenes?

- What kind of work makes you feel most alive?

- What do you see as being your most important work or contribution to the world, whether it's something you are paid for or not?

- Do you enjoy dreaming up things (ideas, programs, projects, items, etc.) and bringing them to fruition, or would you rather work on something that already exists?

- Do you prefer to work in large groups/teams or solo?

- Is there a certain time of day when you feel the most productive?

- Do you find yourself feeling more accomplished when you are writing, researching, or creating?

Now, this isn't something that can be done overnight, it's a process of getting really honest with yourself, reflecting on the various experiences you've had, and determining which ones you would love to do again and which ones you would rather skip.

Once you've been able to dedicate some time and focus to answering these questions honestly, take a few moments to reflect on what you've uncovered and start thinking of specific actions you can take to create more fulfillment and joy in your life.

The other really big piece of uncovering who you are is taking a look at your values. Start by asking yourself the questions below.

- What things do you prioritize above all else?

- What matters most to you?

- What's most important in your life?

- Are you incentivized by the idea of a certain title, a paycheck, a material possession, or a feeling of accomplishment and pride? *For most of us, it's a mix of things, but it's important that you take the time to reflect on what matters most to you.*

- Think about someone you respect and look up to. What are 3 qualities that you admire most about them, and why?

- Looking beyond the physical necessities to live (food, water, air, and shelter) what are 5 things that you require in life to feel fulfilled?

Below is a list of various values; circle or highlight those that are important to you, then take a few moments to journal about what those values mean to you specifically. For example, loyalty to you may mean that when times are hard, or situations sticky, you have someone who remains in your corner, cheering you on, despite everything else that's going on.

Achievement	*Fairness*	*Humor*	*Perseverance*
Ambition	*Faith*	*Inclusiveness*	*Practicality*
Authenticity	*Family*	*Individuality*	*Respect*
Authority	*Friendship*	*Influence*	*Responsibility*
Balance	*Fulfillment*	*Integrity*	*Security*
Change	*Generosity*	*Kindness*	*Self-Sufficiency*
Courage	*Happiness*	*Knowledge*	*Service*
Creativity	*Harmony*	*Learning*	*Teamwork*
Duty	*Health*	*Loyalty*	*Wealth*
Empathy	*Honesty*	*Objectivity*	
Excellence	*Humility*	*Openness*	

By determining what your own non-negotiable values are, you're going to be better positioned to find (or create) the right path for yourself.

_____
_____
_____
_____
_____
_____
_____
_____

Explore

Once you've uncovered the things that matter most to you, it's time to start exploring the options you have available to you. The key here is being open to trying new things.

Growing up, my parents always encouraged me to take calculated risks and chances. They both set a strong example for me of what it means to be the first at something. This doesn't just mean exploring different tasks and positions though, it also means being open to different kinds of people and environments. Imagine how boring life would be if you were always surrounded by people who were exactly like you. Sure, it can be comforting to have a group of friends or colleagues who are similar to yourself, but it's also important to expand our networks to include people who complement our shortcomings, and that we can assist by leaning into our talents.

It's important to remember that we don't always have to agree with everyone else; however, staying open to hearing the opinions, beliefs, and experiences of others can help us develop an even broader understanding of the world around us, strengthening who we are as individuals.

Pursue

This is where the rubber meets the road. Once you've uncovered who you are at your core, what makes you tick, and what you really want to be doing in life and found a few opportunities to explore various options in those areas, it's time to get to work.

This may mean applying for and accepting an internship in a field you'd like to try out. Or, joining a new networking group to expand your connections with other professionals within a certain industry or field. It may mean enrolling in a course that piques your interest, to see if it's an area you'd like to explore further. The big thing here is to remember that you're only trying things on, you haven't made a huge commitment, and if you decide this isn't the right course for you, that's great. You now know something more about yourself, and you can move on to trying the next thing. This is what's considered having a *growth mindset*.

There are those individuals with a *fixed mindset* and those with a *growth mindset*. A fixed mindset is something that can greatly hinder the things a person is able to accomplish in life, both personally and professionally, because of the way it limits what they see as being possible. A growth mindset however means that someone is open to learning from their mistakes, embracing challenges, inspiring others, seeking feedback, testing boundaries, and embracing growth over perfection.

Now, I understand that this may be easier for some than others, and I also recognize that I have some privilege here, in knowing from a young age that I had a solid foundation of support and encouragement from both of my parents. They've always been there for me as a safety net, a sounding board, and a voice of reason. This isn't something that all people have, so for some individuals, this entire process may be much scarier and intimidating; however, I encourage you to remember that no matter what else is going on around you, you always have to bet on yourself. If you don't give yourself permission to try something new, you'll never know what might have happened, what could have been, or what you could have achieved. And a life of regret is never the best option. You deserve more!

Reflect on everything you've already overcome.

Set a timer for 20 minutes and write yourself a letter about all of the challenges you've overcome, the strengths you possess, and the many ways in which you've demonstrated resilience in your life thus far. Now this letter may be more of a bulleted list with details, or a formal letter, there's no right or wrong way to organize this. What matters is that you're taking a few moments to recognize and respect everything that you've already overcome in life. Each and every one of us have experienced times when we've doubted ourselves, our abilities, and yet we've persevered and come out the other side. Remember, this letter is for no one else. Be honest, vulnerable, and really celebrate the incredible person you are.

A few thoughts to help prompt you while writing this letter:

- Think back to specific challenges you've faced - heartbreaks, losses, setbacks, health issues - really any difficult experiences you've encountered. How did you feel in the moment and what specific steps did you take to navigate the challenges?
- Remind yourself of the inner strength and resilience you possess, specifically highlighting the times when you've surprised yourself with your ability to cope, adapt, and overcome.
- How have these challenges shaped you into the person you are today? What lessons have you learned and how have you grown from these experiences?

- Imagine you're writing this letter to someone else - someone you care about greatly. It can often feel easier to give words of support and encouragement to others, than it is to give them to ourselves.

Don't be afraid to talk to people.

I've always had a very close relationship with both of my parents, and I still talk with them about the big things going on in my life, sometimes just sharing exciting achievements, but other times, seeking their advice and opinions on something. I also have an amazing husband whom I can talk to about anything and a close group of friends and colleagues whom I trust. I can go to all these people with anything I may be working through, struggling with, or contemplating.

When you have a close network of people who know you, personally and professionally, they can often see things from a different perspective, providing you with valuable insights into areas that you may have either overlooked or not recognized because you were too close to the situation.

Take a few minutes and jot down some of the people in your life that you feel most comfortable talking to about different aspects of your life. This may be the same few people for all areas of your life, or you may have different people for your personal and professional life.

For law students who may be reading this, don't be afraid to make connections with your professors while in law school. Not only do they have experience teaching, but in the time you're spending together, they will get a pretty good understanding of who you are, how you work, and what areas of the law or otherwise might be best suited for you in the future. You may have natural abilities that you don't recognize yourself and having a professor on your side who can help guide you to options can be a huge help.

Getting to know alumni is also an amazing way to explore different opportunities and ask questions of people who've been exactly where you are right now. As a member of my law school's alumni association board, I especially love it when students reach out to me to ask questions about what I do, how I got into my practice area, and any recommendations I might have for them if they're interested in pursuing a similar path. Similarly, I make myself available to students at my undergraduate school. There's no harm in reaching out and asking if someone is willing to have a quick virtual coffee chat or email exchange with you. You might be surprised at the connections you can make just by staying open and reaching out.

Stay open & curious.

While in college, and then law school, I enrolled in as many classes as possible, sometimes taking up to 21 credits at a time. While I don't necessarily recommend anyone do exactly what I did, I do believe it's important that you give yourself permission to stay curious. Remember, it's okay and expected that you won't love everything you try, but again, when you find something that doesn't light you up, you can move on to trying something new that might.

As you read earlier, since I was young, I wanted to be a doctor. I had grown up hearing about how the most successful people in the world were doctors. To be fair, I know plenty of other amazingly talented and successful people who are in completely different industries, but as a child, being a doctor was what I had my eye on. Once I was in college, I started taking my pre-med courses, but I also filled my schedule with drama classes, astronomy lab, the history of jazz, art history, dream interpretation, history of the civil rights movement with Julian Bond, a ton of government and political science classes with Larry Sabato, and a multitude of other courses. I figured that my time at UVA was my opportunity to explore and try on as many courses as I could. It just so happened that one of those off-topic areas I explored was a commercial law course from the Commerce School and right away, my focus shifted. The things I learned in that single course made sense, they encouraged me to explore a new way of thinking, and just like that, instead of wanting to be a doctor, I wanted to be a lawyer.

But even after I had graduated from law school, I still wasn't sure what kind of lawyer I wanted to be; I had not yet settled on an area of practice. So, I set about exploring even more options within my chosen industry. I took my time, followed my curiosity, and tried different positions, some legal, and some non-legal. It was through that meandering journey that I found the career that interested me. It aligns with my values, meets my needs and non-negotiables, and keeps me busy with fast-paced changes. By staying open and curious, you never know what you might find.

Don't be afraid to say something is NOT right for you.

Finding what isn't right for you is just as important as finding what is. There are always going to be certain roles, industries, and careers that will clash with your values, or what you enjoy spending your time doing. Instead of fighting an uphill battle for potentially 40 years or more in a role or career that never felt right, give yourself permission to say 'no.' The sooner you do this, the sooner you're able to move on, try something else, and find what does light you up.

I knew pretty quickly that there was a certain area of law that was a definite no for me. I did an internship in Miami, Florida the summer before my last year of law school. I had always wanted to live in Miami, and this seemed like the perfect opportunity to check out the area as well as explore a new area of the law that I hadn't before. I already knew that I wasn't interested in spending the summer inside a traditional law firm, so instead, I worked with the Miami-Dade Public Defender's Office.

I was 24, spending my summer in Miami, living in an apartment in Brickell with a friend of a friend, and I thought I was living my best life. However, during my internship, I was exposed to many things I hadn't experienced before, from visiting my first jail to interviewing criminal defendants, and police officers. It was difficult seeing so many people behind bars, in situations that were the last domino in a line of previous offenses, often meaning they're presumed guilty instead of innocent. Something that I struggled with quite a bit despite my belief that you are responsible for your actions.

The lawyers I worked with in Miami had an overwhelming level of passion for their work. It's not like what we see on TV; these are hard-working, devoted public attorneys who work tirelessly for their clients with limited resources, and a seemingly endless caseload. When I came back home after the summer was over, I was extremely grateful for the opportunity and had tremendous respect for the attorneys at the public defender's office. I also knew that I could not do that on a daily basis. However, I never would have known that, had I not taken the chance and tried.

If you're thinking about applying for a clerkship...

While doing a year-long clerkship was a great experience for me, and Judge Lawson helped me in more ways than I can count, a clerkship isn't the right choice for everyone.

I recommend that if you're thinking about applying for a clerkship you will first want to sit down and decide what it is you're hoping to get out of the experience. For me, because I graduated from law school and was still unsure of exactly what I wanted to do next, applying for a clerkship made sense. It provided me with exposure to new areas of the law as well as an amazing mentor who was eager to help answer my questions and guide me.

If you do decide to apply for a clerkship it's important that you research and find the right Judge for what you're hoping to achieve.

- Are you wanting someone willing to go above and beyond to mentor you, not only during your time together but as your career progresses?
- Or are you seeking someone who will help show you the ropes of what they do on a daily basis, and once your clerkship is over, you generally move on?

Neither of these is right or wrong, it just depends on what you personally are looking for. Making the connection with the right Judge can be instrumental in opening doors for your future as well as allowing you to observe the legal proceedings in a community that you may be interested in relocating to. For instance, if you attended law school in one state, but were curious about living and working in a different state, you may choose to apply for a clerkship in that different state. That way, before you make a long-term commitment to move somewhere, you have a chance to meet the local attorneys, familiarize yourself with the different firms and legal community there, and get a sense of how the lawyers there function. You get to determine if an area meets your values and non-negotiables, and if it doesn't, your position is only temporary and you have the freedom to try something else, somewhere else.

Always invest in yourself.

Even if the company or organization you're working for, or involved with, does not pay for conferences, webinars, or professional development programs, if there is something out there that you want to do, that you believe will benefit you and your career in the long run, spend your money and use your time to make it happen. It's always a good idea to bet on yourself. I've been fortunate that many organizations I have been with have paid for off-site trainings, conferences, or for me to attend virtual webinars or be a part of month-long personal development programs. But not all have. For those that haven't, I have chosen to invest in myself and paid my own way or joined the speaker faculty or board to receive complimentary registration. Either way, I made sure I was there to stay engaged in my industry, to stay up to date with trends and best practices in the marketplace, and to continue to strengthen and grow my network. It's up to you to succeed. Your life and career will be what you make of it.

At the end of the day, what matters most is that you're giving yourself the time needed to discover what your personal values are, find the ways in which you want to make a difference - an impact - in the world, and make a plan to pursue your chosen path towards your own purpose-filled life.

Michelle Trong Perrin-Steinberg

Key Takeaways

- **Embrace Others:** Growing up as a biracial child in a military family, I often felt different. My experiences taught me the importance of creating a sense of belonging, connection, and growth for everyone, which has become a driving force in my life and career. In what areas of your life have you felt different? How can you better embrace those differences?

- **Adaptability and Openness:** Moving frequently and living in various cultures as part of a military family helped me develop adaptability and flexibility. These experiences shaped my ability to connect with new people and environments, emphasizing the value of understanding and embracing differences. In what areas of your life can you better practice being adaptable and open to new possibilities and experiences?

- **The Power of Support and Sacrifice:** Witnessing my parent's sacrifices to help our extended family taught me that family, community, and helping others should come first. This mindset has shaped my approach to life, focusing on building bridges and creating opportunities for others. What does your support system look like? This may be family, friends, coworkers, etc. What sacrifices have been made in order to support you in your endeavors?

- **Finding Joy in Connection:** Music, books, and shared experiences have always been ways for me to connect with others. I've learned that building relationships is one of the most powerful tools for personal growth and creating lasting bonds with those around us. What are some things that you enjoy doing? How can you lean into those interests to form connections with others?

- **Resilience and Determination Lead to Success:** Both of my parents demonstrated that with resilience, hard work, and determination, I can overcome obstacles and achieve great things, regardless of the challenges I might face. Their life examples taught me that it's possible to make the seemingly impossible a reality by never giving up and believing in myself. Where in your life might you be facing a challenge? How might you be able to better show your own resilience and determination toward achieving your dreams?

- **Value of Humility and Kindness:** Even in their pursuit of dreams and achievements, my parents emphasized the importance of staying humble and treating others with kindness. They showed me that true success is not just about personal accomplishments but also about respecting and valuing those around me. How are you currently showing kindness to others? What is one small thing you can do today, to show kindness and compassion for someone in your life? Or how might you be able to show kindness to a stranger?

- **Financial Responsibility and Life Lessons:** From a young age, I was taught the value of financial responsibility and the importance of budgeting. This lesson shaped my understanding of making mindful financial decisions and planning for the future, which has had a lasting impact on my life. Do you feel confident in your financial responsibility? Do you currently set up a budget for yourself, your household expenses, and future planning? If not, what is one thing you can do today to take a step towards financial stability?

- **Choosing a Supportive Life Partner:** My parent's relationship demonstrated the significance of choosing a life partner who supports your dreams and ambitions. Following their example, I found a partner in my own husband, who not only respects and understands my goals but also shares responsibilities, allowing me to thrive in both my career and family life. Do you currently have a partner or significant other? How do they support your dreams and ambitions? How are you able to support theirs?

- **Embrace Change and Keep Moving Forward:** It's okay to change your mind and pursue a different career path if your interests shift. Trust in your ability to learn and adapt to new challenges, even if it means stepping into unfamiliar territory. Keep an open mind and be willing to explore different roles, industries, and experiences. Each position you take on, even if it's not your ultimate passion, can provide valuable lessons that contribute to your overall growth and success. Are you feeling confident and excited about your current career path? If not, are you open to change and trying something new? Do you have any ideas of what you might like to pursue or try instead?

- **Building Relationships Is Key:** Developing strong relationships and networking with others is crucial for growth and success. A supportive professional network can provide guidance, and opportunities to help you achieve your goals. Do you currently have a network that you can go to for advice, feedback, and support? If not, how can you go about building a network?

- **Representation and Inclusion Matter:** It's crucial to have greater representation of women and people of color in leadership positions, not only in the legal industry but all industries. Diverse perspectives bring value, challenge the status quo, and open up new opportunities for individuals and the communities they serve. Speak up. Your voice deserves recognition.

- **Own Your Journey:** Believing in yourself, staying true to your values, and not letting others define your limits are keys to success. It's important to have a plan, stay motivated, and surround yourself with supportive people who will encourage you to reach for your dreams. Who is currently on your dream team? These are the people who support and encourage you throughout your journey, no matter what.

- **Know Yourself:** Understanding who you are at your core is the foundation for a fulfilling life. Take the time to explore your passions, values, and the things that truly make you feel alive. Reflect on your experiences to identify what you enjoy and what doesn't resonate with you.

- **Embrace Exploration in Your 20s:** Your 20s are a time for self-discovery and growth. Use this period to try new things, explore different interests, and take risks. Don't limit yourself based on others' expectations—focus on finding what excites and energizes you.

- **Adopt a Growth Mindset:** Be open to learning from your experiences and mistakes. A growth mindset encourages you to embrace challenges, seek feedback, and stay curious about new possibilities. It's okay to realize that something isn't right for you and move on to explore new paths.

- **Invest in Yourself:** Always bet on yourself by pursuing opportunities for growth, even if it means investing your own time or money. Prioritize continuous learning, networking, and personal development to create a life and career that aligns with your values and aspirations.

Additional Resources

- [Women, Influence & Power in Law (WIPL)](#) Annual Conference - Described as one of the "most inspiring and empowering women's conferences in the legal space," WIPL offers an opportunity for unprecedented exchange with women in-house and outside counsel.

- [Legal Speak Podcast](#) - Legal Speak is a weekly podcast that makes sense of what's happening in the legal industry. Each episode, while only a few minutes long, tackles a subject that's worthy of a deep dive and provides valuable insights from industry experts.

- [Association of Corporate Counsel (ACC)](#) - ACC is a global bar association that promotes the common professional and business interests of in-house counsel through information, education, networking opportunities, and advocacy initiatives.

- [Corporate Counsel Women of Color (CCWC)](#) - Corporate Counsel Women of Color was founded in 2004 with the mission to foster diversity, equity, and inclusion in the legal profession. Today, CCWC is the nation's largest organization for corporate in-house women of color attorneys.

- [Society for International Affairs (SIA)](#) - SIA, is a volunteer, non-profit, educational organization that was jointly formed in 1967 by US Government and Industry. SIA provides a forum for the exchange of information related to export and import licensing. SIA interests cover the entire spectrum of licensing and compliance issues pertaining to the Departments of Commerce, Defense, State, and Treasury.

- Berkeley Law Executive Education General Counsel University - General Counsel University ("GC University") is an online course and community that provides legal professionals with the critical skills needed to become a general counsel (GC) or be hired and retained by GCs. Designed by leading GCs from world-class companies, the program demystifies the intricate nature of the legal department's role in an organization. *I received a scholarship to join the inaugural cohort program and completed the course in October 2024.*

- McKinsey Connected Leaders Academy - Connected Leaders Academy is a training program to help organizations make demonstrable progress on inclusion and equity, improve talent pipelines, and unlock the full potential of people within the company. This program includes customized content relevant to Black, Hispanic/Latino, and Asian leaders—and focuses on early professionals, mid-career managers, and senior executives. *I was nominated for the management program and completed it in early 2024.*

- Management Leadership for Tomorrow, Career Advancement Program (MLT CAP) - Learn what it takes to advance to the C-Suite. Navigating from mid-career professional to senior executive may be the most challenging part of your career journey. You are confident you have what it takes to be an effective and successful leader, but the path to career advancement can be filled with personal and professional roadblocks. This 9-month program provides highly talented, mid-career professionals with the keys to unlock their full potential and advance toward senior leadership roles in their respective organizations. *I was nominated for this program and completed it in early 2024.*

- [Sparktype Assessment](#) - Your Sparketype™ is the essential nature of work that fills you with meaning and lets you feel fully expressed, alive with purpose, and absorbed in flow. Your Sparketype serves as one of the single biggest clues in your quest to figure out what to do with your life. You can dig into uncovering your own Sparketype details either via the website or the book.

About the Author

Michelle Trong Perrin-Steinberg has 20 years of leadership experience as a lawyer leading high-performing teams and spearheading global training programs in various industries including technology; aerospace and defense; higher-education; traditional law firm; and Big 4 consulting. Outside of work, Michelle is dedicated to mentoring and advancing women and underrepresented groups in the legal profession.

Michelle currently calls Oahu, Hawaii home, where she enjoys island life with her husband, their young son, and active Goldendoodle; however, soon, the family will be moving to the south to be closer to immediate and extended family.

For more information visit her website - www.michelletrongperrinsteinberg.com.

Michelle Trong Perrin-Steinberg

Kindly, Michelle

Acknowledgment

This book would not have been published if it were not for Megs Thompson. Megs, thank you for your support in brainstorming, organizing, and editing this book. We've had weekly calls, shared many emails (to multiple accounts), had Zoom video calls, exchanged a ton of texts and had a lot of laughter and fun along the way. I know we were meant to meet one another and I am so happy we did. I am incredibly grateful to you. Thank you, Megs.

Michelle Trong Perrin-Steinberg

Milton Keynes UK
Ingram Content Group UK Ltd.
UKHW020850111124
451035UK00011B/890

9 781961 185692